ESSENTIAL ELEMENTS

FOR STRINGS

A COMPREHENSIVE STRING METHOD

By
Michael Allen • Robert Gillespie • Pamela Tellejohn Hayes
Arrangements by John Higgins

CONGRATULATIONS and WELCOME to Book 2 of Essential Elements for Strings!

By now you are well aware of the benefits and joy of playing the violin in the orchestra. Book 2 will help you to reach a more advanced level, and your musical experiences will become even more fun and exciting.

But remember, all of the techniques you learned and practiced in Book 1, especially instrument position, left hand shape, and fingerings and bowings, are even more important now. These skills need to be refined, and in order to progress, you must continue to practice carefully and regularly.

There will be rewards for your effort! As you spend time learning more challenging material, the mastery of new skills will bring you even more joy in the years to come. Good luck and best wishes for a lifetime of musical happiness!

ISBN 0-7935-4297-9

HAL•LEONARD™
CORPORATION
7777 W. BLUEMOUND RD. P.O. BOX 13819 MILWAUKEE, WI 53213

00862549

2

 **Major Scale**   A Major Scale is a series of eight notes that follow a definite pattern of whole steps and half steps. Half steps appear only between scale steps 3-4 and 7-8. Every major scale has the same arrangement of whole steps and half steps.

1. D MAJOR SCALE - Round

2. D MAJOR MANIA

3. D MAJOR DUET

4. DOTTED HALF REVIEW   Mark the half steps before you play.

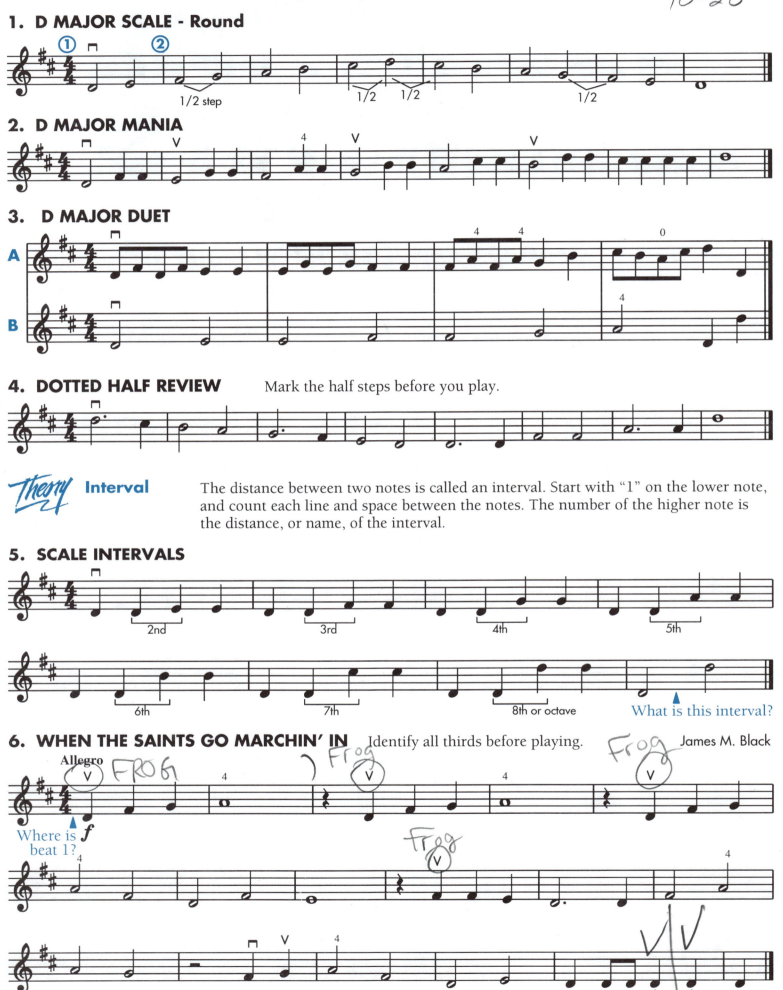

 **Interval**   The distance between two notes is called an interval. Start with "1" on the lower note, and count each line and space between the notes. The number of the higher note is the distance, or name, of the interval.

5. SCALE INTERVALS

What is this interval?

6. WHEN THE SAINTS GO MARCHIN' IN   Identify all thirds before playing.   James M. Black

Allegro

Where is beat 1?

7. G MAJOR SCALE - Round

8. UPPER DECK   Remember to count.

9. G MAJOR ARPEGGIOS - Duet   Identify all fourths before playing.

Dynamics   crescendo (cresc.)   Gradually increase volume.
decrescendo (decresc.)   Gradually decrease volume.

10. DYNAMIC CONTRASTS

Ritardando   (ritard.) (rit.)   Gradually slow the tempo.

11. POLISH CAROL   Eastern European Folk Song

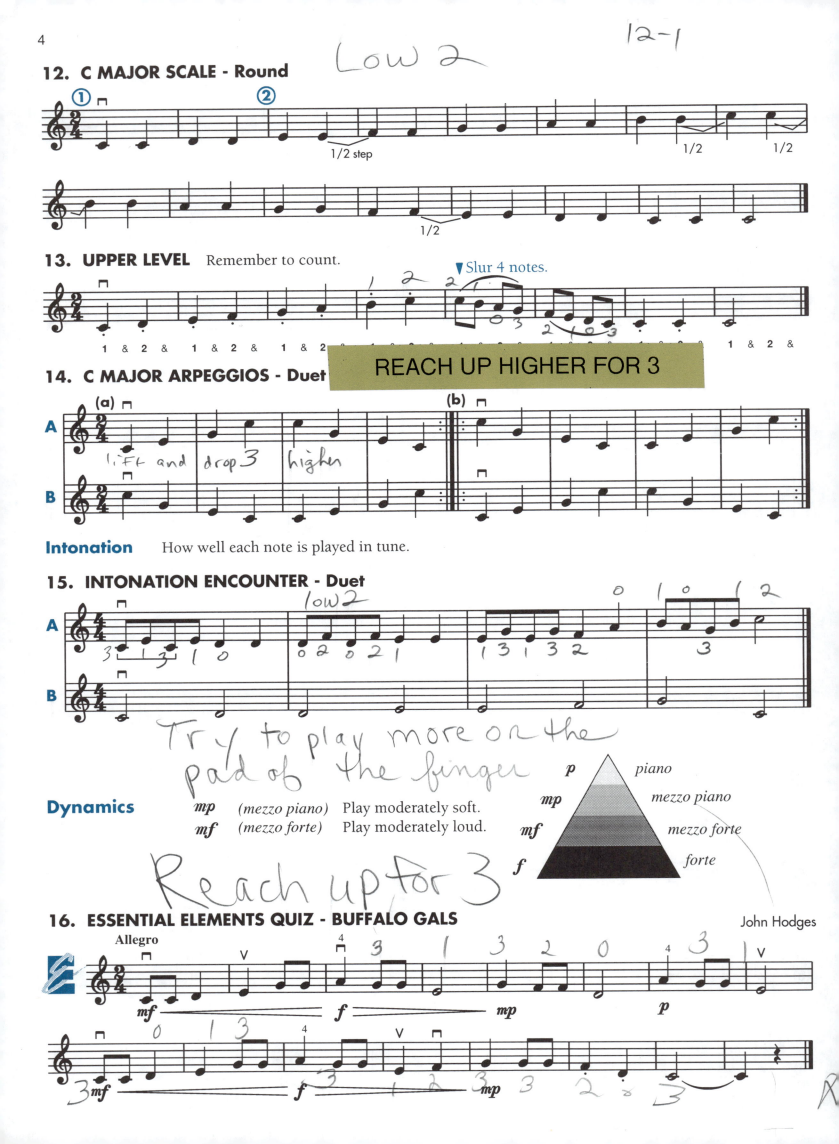

17. SALSA SIESTA - Duet

Allegretto ◄ A lively tempo, faster than *Andante,* but slower than *Allegro.*

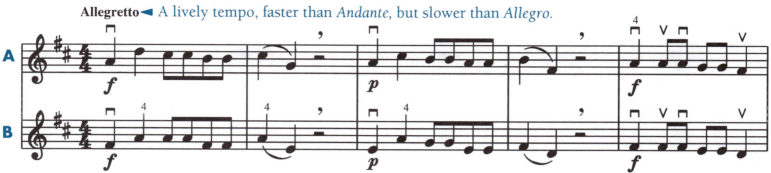

Tunneling
Slide your fingers up and down the fingerboard between 2 strings.

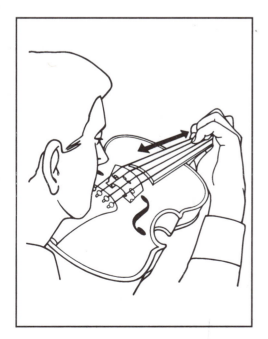

Ridin' The Rails
Slide up and down one string with your fingers.

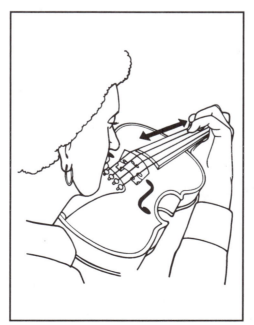

Tappin' And Slidin'
Tap your fingers on any string, slide toward the other end of the fingerboard, and tap again.

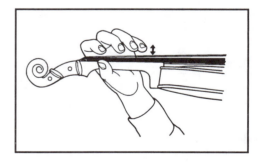

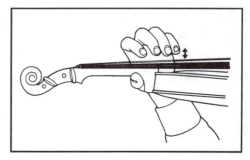

History Jesse James (1847-1882) was an outlaw and gunslinger. He made his living by robbing banks and trains throughout Missouri and Kansas. No. 26. *Jesse James* is an American folk song about this Robin Hood legend who helped the poor. During his lifetime, French impressionistic painters Edouard Manet and Claude Monet created some of their most famous paintings, author Herman Melville wrote *Moby Dick,* and Lewis Carroll wrote *Alice in Wonderland.*

26. ESSENTIAL ELEMENTS QUIZ - JESSE JAMES
American Folk Song

Sightreading Playing a musical selection for the first time is called sightreading. The key to sightreading success is to know what to look for before playing the piece. Follow the guidelines below, and your orchestra will be sightreading STARS! Use the word **STARS** to remind yourself what to look for before reading a selection the first time.

S — Sharps or flats in the **key signature**   Identify the key signature first. Silently practice notes from the key signature. Look for key signature changes in the piece.
T — Time signature and **tempo markings**   Identify and look for changes in the piece.
A — Accidentals   Check for any sharps, flats, or naturals not found in the key signature.
R — Rhythm   Slowly count and shadow bow all difficult rhythms. Pay special attention to rests.
S — Signs   Look for all signs that indicate bowings, dynamics, tempo changes, repeats, 1st and 2nd endings, and any other instructions printed on your music.

27. SIGHTREADING CHALLENGE #1   Remember to count.

28. SIGHTREADING CHALLENGE #2

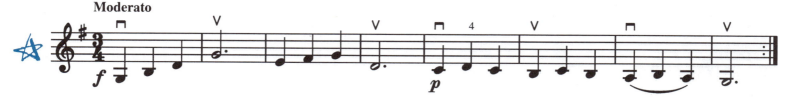

29. SIGHTREADING CHALLENGE #3

Review Work-outs on page 5 daily.

8

**Dotted Quarter Note
Eighth Note** = 2 Beats

Remember, a dot adds half the value of the note.

Remember, a single eighth note has a flag on the stem.

Flag

30. RHYTHM RAP

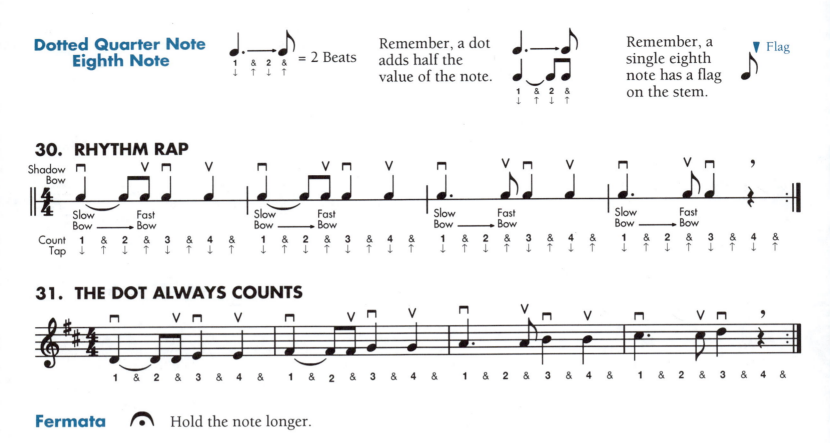

31. THE DOT ALWAYS COUNTS

Fermata Hold the note longer.

32. G MAJOR BONANZA - Duet

33. RHYTHM RAP

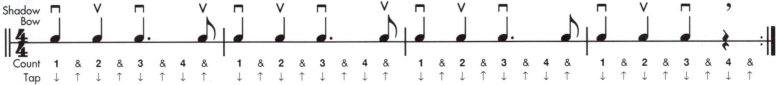

34. C MAJOR SEQUENCE

History

Chorales are German hymns or songs that were first written by **Martin Luther** (1483-1546) to help people sing together during church services. While Luther was writing his chorales, Michelangelo began painting the ceiling in the Sistine Chapel in Rome (1508), and Ponce de Leon discovered Florida (1513). The *St. Anthony Chorale* is attributed to the great Austrian composer **Franz Joseph Haydn** (1732-1809).

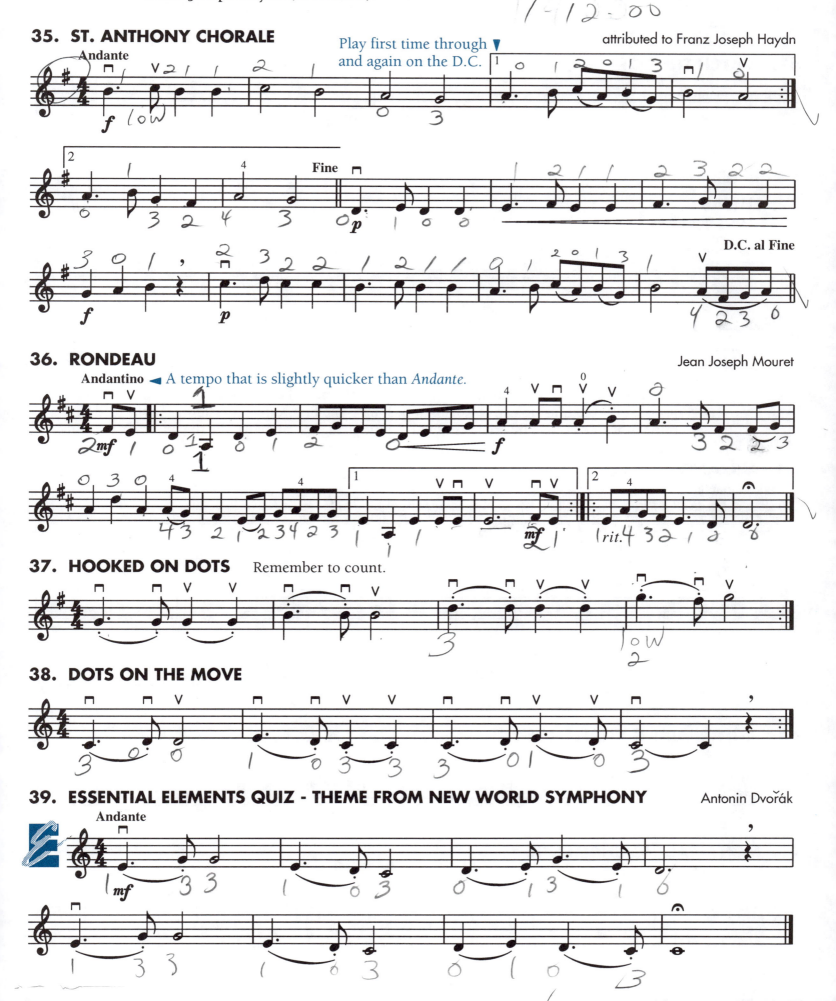

10

Legato Play in a smooth and connected style.

40. SMOOTH CONNECTIONS

41. WATCH THE DOT

Fast Slow Bow Bow
Fast Slow Bow Bow

e ■ The Italian word for "and".

42. LULLABY

Johannes Brahms

Andante e legato

Early **Korean music** was influenced by the music of China, but eventually developed its own special style, often using native Korean folk songs. The first Korean music was performed in the courts of Korea's rulers by orchestras with exotic string instruments like the *haekeum, komungo,* and the *kayakeum* - an instrument which had 12 bridges!

43. ARIRANG

Korean Folk Song

Andante

44. SIGHTREADING CHALLENGE #4 Review the **STARS** guidelines before sightreading (p.7).

Moderato

45. SIGHTREADING CHALLENGE #5

Andante

Key Change Sometimes a key signature will change in the middle of a piece of music. You will usually see a thin double bar line at a key change. Keep going, making sure you are playing all the correct notes in the new signature.

46. WHERE, OH WHERE IS MY KEY?

47. AMERICA THE BEAUTIFUL - Orchestra Arrangement

Samuel Augustus Ward
Arr. John Higgins

A = Melody. **B** = Harmony. For orchestral playing, half of the violins play each part.

Continue reviewing Work-outs on page 5.

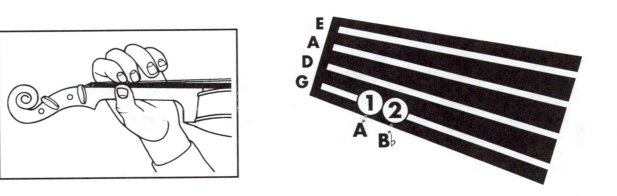

B♭ is played with low 2nd finger on the G string.

Listening Skills Play what your teacher plays. Listen carefully.

2 – 2

48. LET'S READ "B♭" (B-flat)

49. VIKING WAY

Team Work Great musicians give encouragement to their fellow performers. Bass players will now learn a new challenging skill. The success of your orchestra depends on everyone's talent and patience. Play your best as members of this section advance their musical technique.

SPECIAL VIOLIN EXERCISE

Draw a note next to each printed note that will match the interval number shown. The note you draw can be higher or lower than the printed note. The first one is done for you.

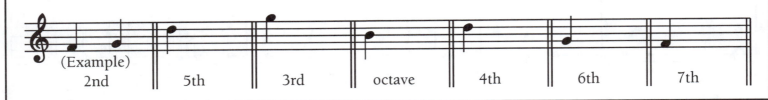

(Example) 2nd   5th   3rd   octave   4th   6th   7th

50. CAVALIER COUNTRY

51. F MAJOR SCALE

F MAJOR Key Signature
Play all B's as **B♭** (B-flat).

History

A **Concerto** is a composition in several movements for solo instrument and orchestra. No. 52. *Theme from Violin Concerto* is from the first movement of *Violin Concerto* for violin and orchestra by **Ludwig van Beethoven** (1770-1827), composed while author William Wordsworth was creating some of his works. A special feature of the concerto is the *cadenza,* a section of the concerto that is improvised, or made up, by the soloist during a concert. Improvising and creating your own music is great fun. Jazz players do it all the time. Try it if you have not already.

52. THEME FROM VIOLIN CONCERTO
Ludwig van Beethoven

53. ECHO-LOGICAL
Remember to count.

54. ESSENTIAL ELEMENTS QUIZ - A CAPITAL SHIP
American Folk Song

55. SIGHTREADING CHALLENGE #6
Review the **STARS** guidelines before sightreading.

56. SIGHTREADING CHALLENGE #7

A NEW FINGER PATTERN - Low 1st Finger

Step 1 - Shape your left hand as shown. Be certain your palm faces you. Notice that there is a space between all four fingers.

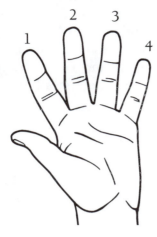

Step 2 - Bring your hand to the fingerboard. There is a space between your 1st and 2nd fingers, between your 2nd and 3rd fingers and between your 3rd and 4th fingers.

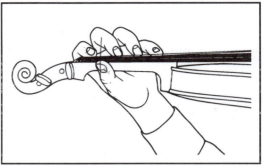

B♭

is played with low 1st finger on the A string.

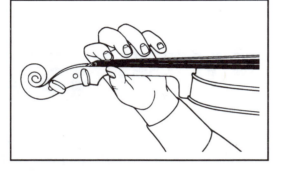

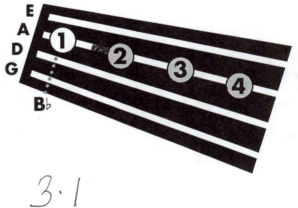

 Play what your teacher plays. Listen carefully. *3·1*

57. LET'S READ "B♭" (B-flat)

58. ROLLING ALONG

Moderato

59. MATCHING OCTAVES

60. TRUMPET VOLUNTARY IN F

Henry Purcell

Andantino

F

is played with
low 1st finger
on the E string.

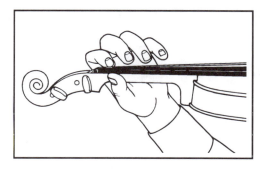

 Play what your teacher plays. Listen carefully.

3·1

61. LET'S READ "F" (F-natural)

62. TECHNIQUE TRAX

63. F MAJOR SCALE   Remember to count.

64. MORE TECHNIQUE TRAX

65. THIRDS IN F MAJOR

66. SILVER MOON

Chinese Folk Song

Lento ◄ Very slow tempo

Alert: This piece has B♭'s **and** E♮'s.

67. ESSENTIAL ELEMENTS QUIZ - AMERICAN PATROL

F.W. Meacham

Allegro

Theory — **Minor Scales**

A **minor scale** is a series of eight notes which follow a definite pattern of whole steps and half steps. The three forms of the minor scale are natural minor, harmonic minor, and melodic minor. The D minor (*natural*) scale uses the same pitches as the F major scale.

68. D MINOR (Natural) SCALE

Scale Steps: 1 2 3 4 5 6 7 8 7 6 5 4 3 2 1

1/2 step   1/2   1/2   1/2

History — German composer **Gustav Mahler** (1860-1911) was also a successful conductor. He believed in unifying the arts and often combined music, poetry, and philosophy in his compositions. No. 69. *Mahler's Theme* first appears in his *Symphony No. 1*, played as a solo by the double bass. During Mahler's lifetime Vincent van Gogh created his most famous paintings, and Mark Twain wrote *Tom Sawyer*.

69. MAHLER'S THEME - Round

Gustav Mahler

Andante

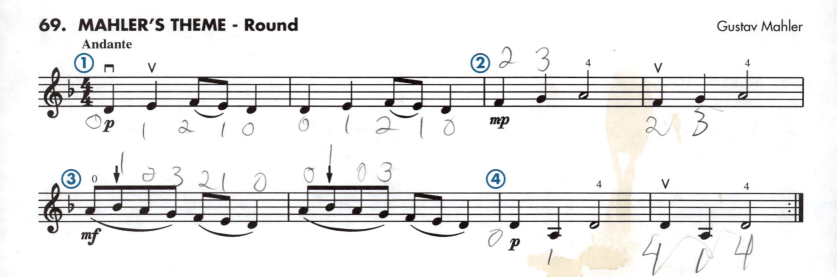

70. SHALOM CHAVERIM

Hebrew Folk Song

71. HOME ON THE RANGE

4-13

Dr. Brewster Higley
Daniel E. Kelley

Gustav Holst (1874-1934) was a famous British orchestra composer who frequently set words to music, including poems by the American poet, Walt Whitman. Holst's *St. Paul's Suite* for string orchestra was written for the St. Paul's Girls School Orchestra and published in 1913. His best known work is *The Planets,* first performed in 1918, the same year as the end of World War I.

72. IN THE BLEAK MIDWINTER - Orchestra Arrangement

4-13

Gustav Holst
Arr. John Higgins

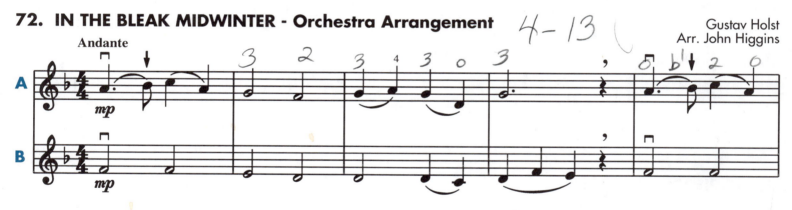

A NEW FINGER PATTERN - High 3rd Finger

Step 1 - Shape your left hand as shown. Be certain your palm faces you. Notice that your 3rd finger lightly touches your 4th finger.

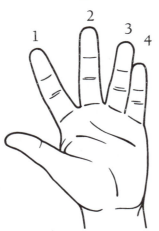

Step 2 - Bring your hand to the fingerboard. Your 3rd and 4th fingers touch. There is a space between your 1st and 2nd fingers and between your 2nd and 3rd fingers.

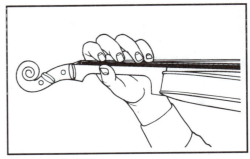

C#

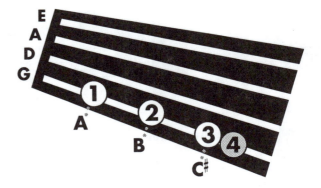

is played with high 3rd finger on the G string.

 Play what your teacher plays. Listen carefully.

4-18

4-13

73. LET'S READ "C#" (C-sharp)

74. AT PIERROT'S DOOR

Andante

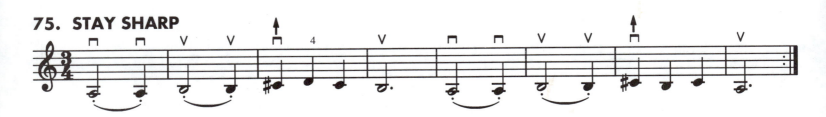

75. STAY SHARP

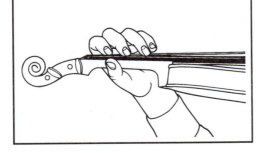

76. HOT CROSS BUNS

Moderato

HIGH THIRD FINGER ON THE D STRING

Shape your hand on the D string as shown.

G♯

is played with
high 3rd finger
on the D string.

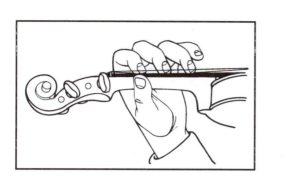

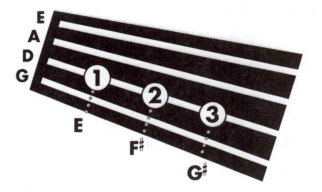

 *Listening Skills* — Play what your teacher plays. Listen carefully.

4-18

77. LET'S READ "G♯" (G-sharp)

78. REACHING OUT

79. HIGHER AND HIGHER

80. A MAJOR SCALE — **A MAJOR Key Signature**

Play all F's as **F♯** (F-sharp), C's as **C♯** (C-sharp), and G's as **G♯** (G-sharp).

81. AYN KAYLOKAYNU

Return to original tempo. ▼ Traditional Jewish Song

Andantino

A Tempo

rit.

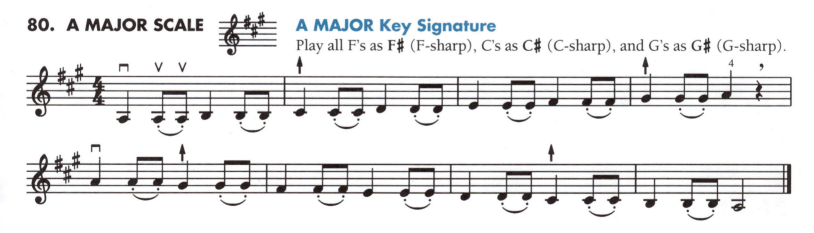

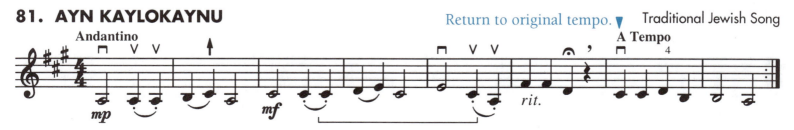

 **Meter Change** Occasionally the meter (time signature) changes in music. Watch for meter changes and count carefully.

82. RHYTHM RAP

83. KUM BA YAH Remember to count. *African Spiritual*

84. FRENCH FOLK SONG

85. SWEET BETSY FROM PIKE *North American Folk Song*

5-3

86. RASA SAYANG EH
Far Eastern Folk Song

87. THE MOUNTAIN DEER CHASE
North American Folk Song

88. ESSENTIAL ELEMENTS QUIZ - MORNING HAS BROKEN
Irish Folk Song

89. SIGHTREADING CHALLENGE #8
Review the **STARS** guidelines before sightreading.

90. SIGHTREADING CHALLENGE #9

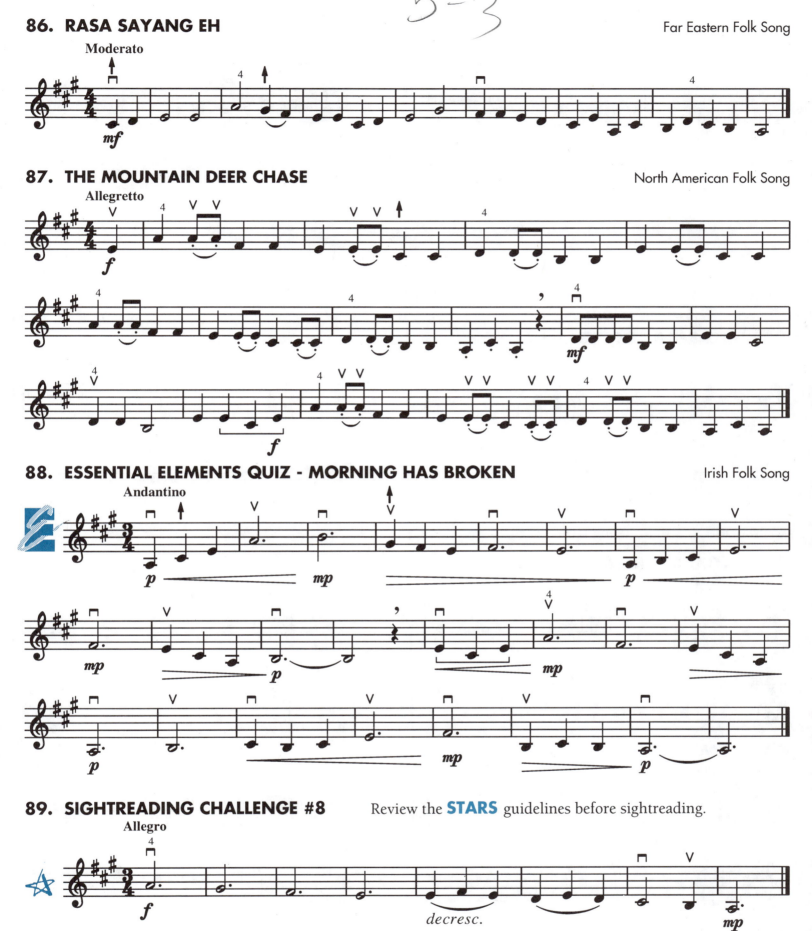
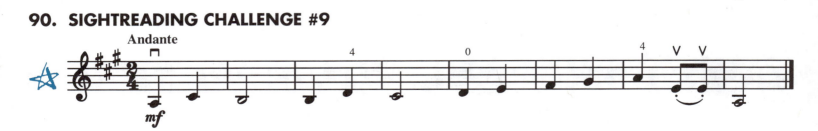

22

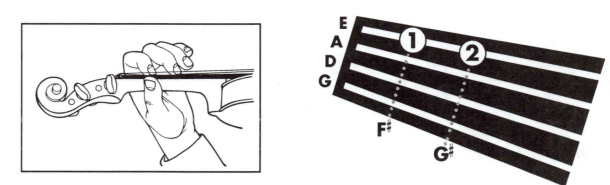

G♯
is played with 2
fingers on the E
string.

Listening Skills Play what your teacher plays. Listen carefully. 6–7

91. LET'S READ "G♯" (G-sharp)

92. A MAJOR SCALE

Cantabile In a singing style.

93. DUTCH CHORALE
Moderato e cantabile

94. SITKA CITY Remember to count. Russian Folk Song
Moderato

95. ESSENTIAL ELEMENTS QUIZ - THE FIG TREE
Allegretto

Alert: This piece has G♯'s **and** D♮'s.

96. LAS MAÑANITAS
Mexican Folk Song

97. ARKANSAS TRAVELER - Orchestra Arrangement
American Folk Song
Arr. John Higgins

Continue reviewing Work-outs on page 5.

SPECIAL VIOLIN EXERCISE

While the violas and cellos learn a new note, draw the bar lines in the music below. Then write in the counting.

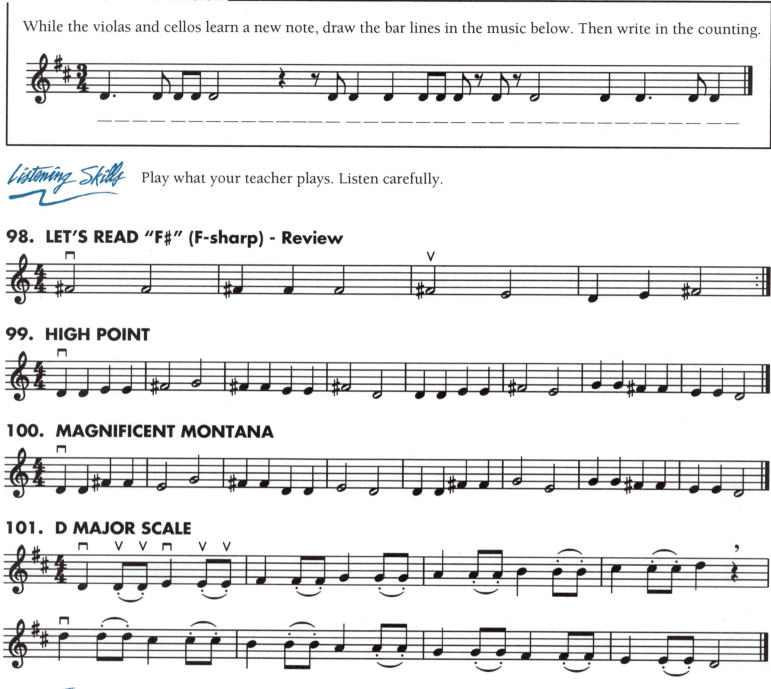

Listening Skills Play what your teacher plays. Listen carefully.

98. LET'S READ "F#" (F-sharp) - Review

99. HIGH POINT

100. MAGNIFICENT MONTANA

101. D MAJOR SCALE

History **Cantatas** are pieces much like short operas that were written during the Baroque Period (1600-1750). They involve vocal soloists and choirs that are accompanied by small orchestras. **Johann Sebastian Bach** (1685-1750) is considered the master of the cantata, and he wrote nearly 300 of them between 1704 and 1745. His "Peasant Cantata" was composed in 1742 when he was living in Leipzig, Germany. While Bach was composing his cantatas, the famous philosopher Voltaire was writing his books and Thomas Jefferson, the great United States president, was born.

102. MARCH FROM PEASANT'S CANTATA

Johann Sebastian Bach

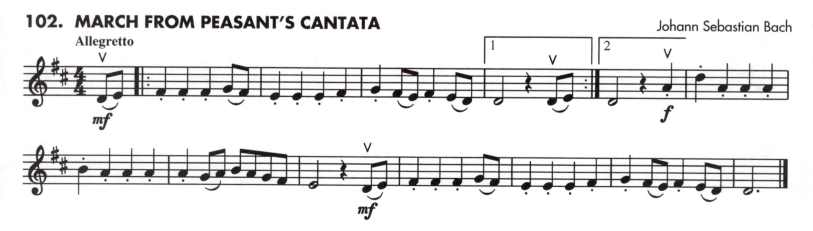

103. ODE TO JOY

Ludwig van Beethoven

Andantino e legato

History In the second half of the 1800s many composers tried to express the spirit of their own country by writing music with a distinct national flavor. Listen to the music of Scandinavian and Spanish composers, and Russians such as Borodin, Tchaikovsky and Rimsky-Korsakov. They often used folk songs and dance rhythms to convey their nationalism.

104. RUSSIAN FOLK TUNE

Allegretto

105. BOTANY BAY   Remember to count.

Australian Folk Song

Moderato

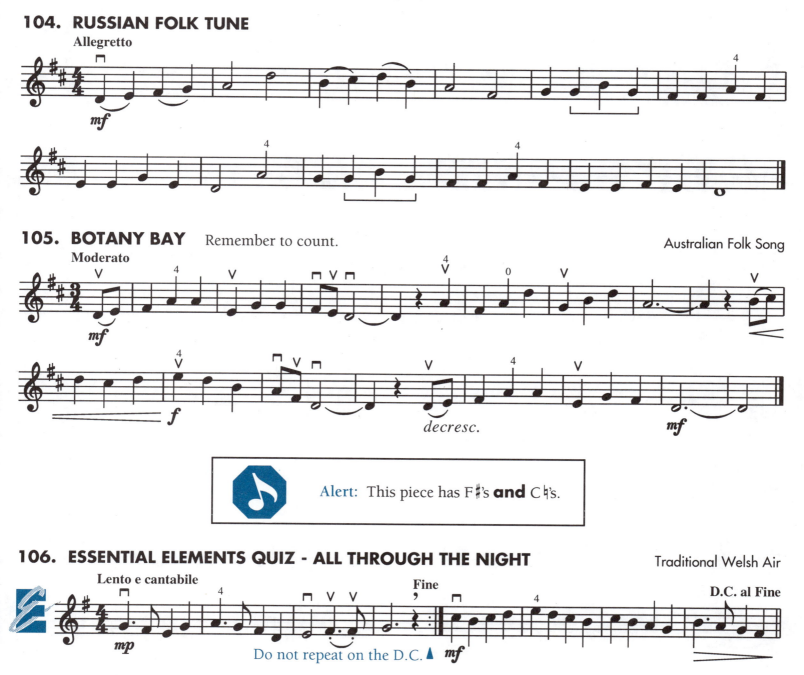

Alert: This piece has F♯'s **and** C♮'s.

106. ESSENTIAL ELEMENTS QUIZ - ALL THROUGH THE NIGHT

Traditional Welsh Air

Lento e cantabile   **Fine**   **D.C. al Fine**

Do not repeat on the D.C. ▲

26

Sixteenth Notes 4 sixteenth notes = 1 beat

A single sixteenth note has 2 flags on the stem.

6-21

107. RHYTHM RAP

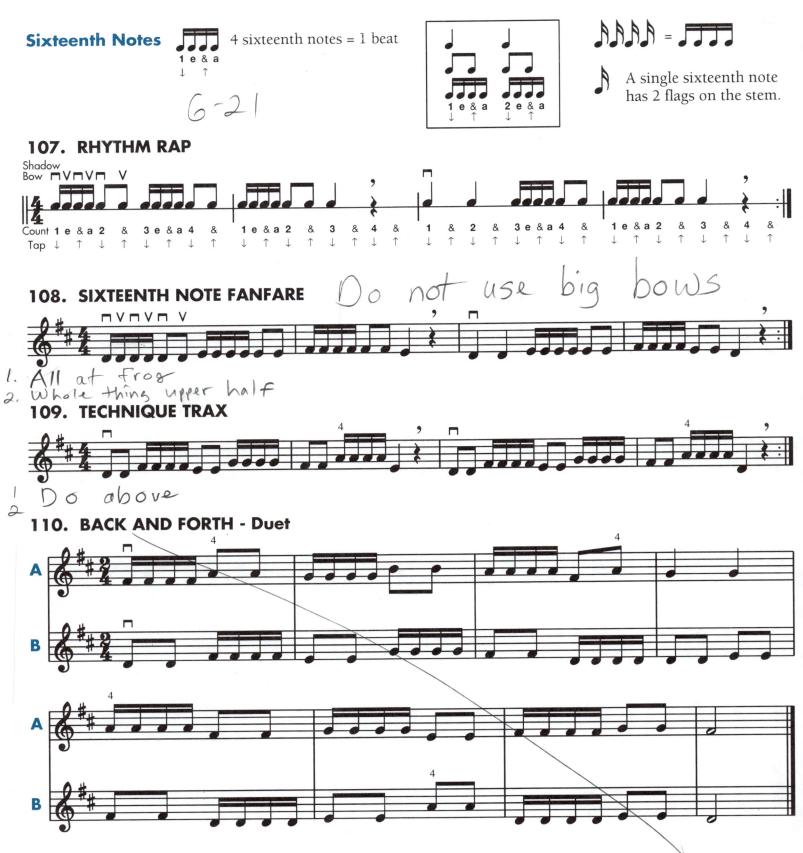

108. SIXTEENTH NOTE FANFARE   Do not use big bows

1. All at frog
2. Whole thing upper half

109. TECHNIQUE TRAX

Do above

110. BACK AND FORTH - Duet

111. MOCKINGBIRD   Remember to count.

Alice Hawthorne

Moderato

6-28

112. RHYTHM RAP

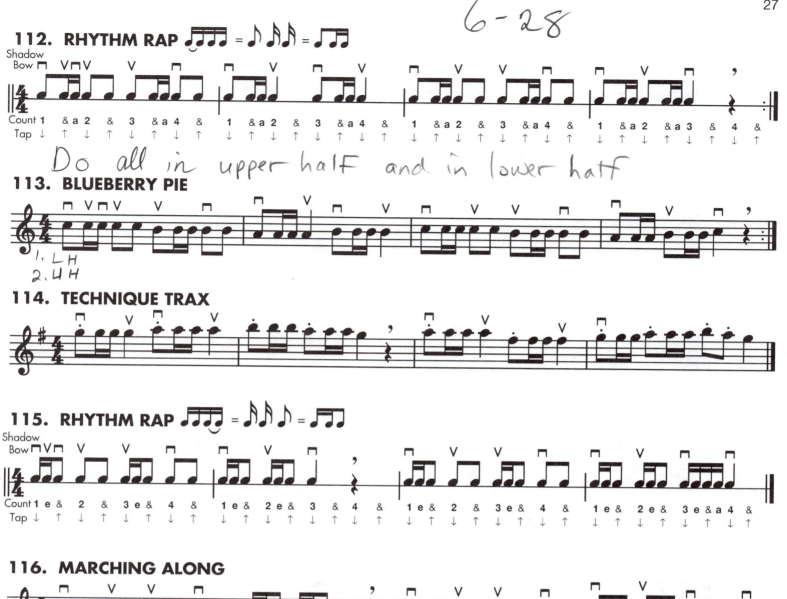

Do all in upper half and in lower half

113. BLUEBERRY PIE

1. LH
2. UH

114. TECHNIQUE TRAX

115. RHYTHM RAP

116. MARCHING ALONG

117. ON THE MOVE

118. RHYTHM ETUDE - Duet

A

B

119. ESSENTIAL ELEMENTS QUIZ - RHYTHM ROUND-UP

6-28

120. RHYTHM RAP

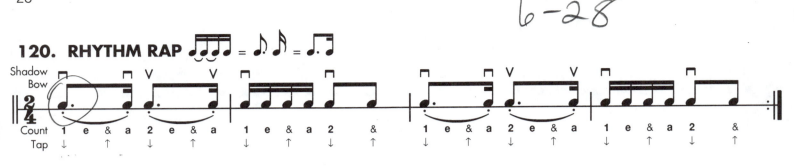

121. TECHNIQUE TRAX

122. HOOKED ON D MAJOR

123. HOOKED AGAIN

124. THE MOUNTAIN CLIMBER

125. SIGHTREADING CHALLENGE #10   Review the **STARS** guidelines before sightreading.

Henry Purcell (1659-1695) was a singer and organist who became one of the most famous composers in the 17th century in England. He composed music for many plays that were performed in schools throughout England, including his famous opera *Dido and Aeneas* in 1689. While Purcell was composing his music in England, New Amsterdam became New York (1664), and Philadelphia was founded by William Penn (1682).

Theory **Syncopation** In many types of music, the emphasis occurs on notes that do not normally receive a strong pulse or beat. This is called **syncopation** and is very common in jazz, rock, and pop, as well as in classical music.

129. RHYTHM RAP

130. SYNCOPATION TIME

131. CHILDREN'S SHOES

Black American Spiritual

132. HOOKED ON SYNCOPATION

133. TOM DOOLEY

American Folk Song

134. SLOVAKIAN FOLK SONG

135. ESSENTIAL ELEMENTS QUIZ - LUCKY LARRY

136. SIGHTREADING CHALLENGE #11   Review the **STARS** guidelines before sightreading.

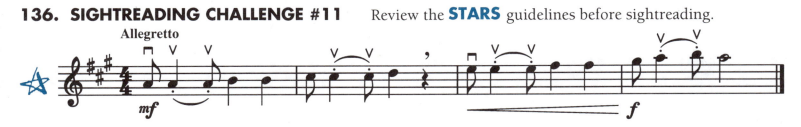

137. SIGHTREADING CHALLENGE #12

138. POMP AND CIRCUMSTANCE - Orchestra Arrangement

Edward Elgar
Arr. John Higgins

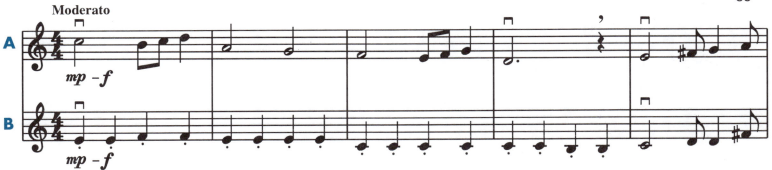

LOW FIRST FINGER ON THE D STRING

Shape your left hand on the D string as shown.

is played with
low 1st finger
on the D string.

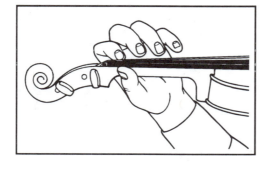

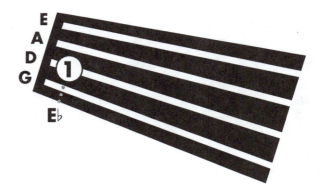

Listening Skills   Play what your teacher plays. Listen carefully.

139. LET'S READ "E♭" (E-flat)

140. UP AND DOWN

141. HIKING ALONG

142. B♭ MAJOR SCALE   **B♭ MAJOR Key Signature**
Play all B's as **B♭** (B-flat) and all E's as **E♭** (E-flat).

143. THE RAKES OF MALLOW   Before playing, mark arrows over all notes played with   Irish Folk Song
low 1st fingers. Then circle all other 1st finger notes.

Allegretto

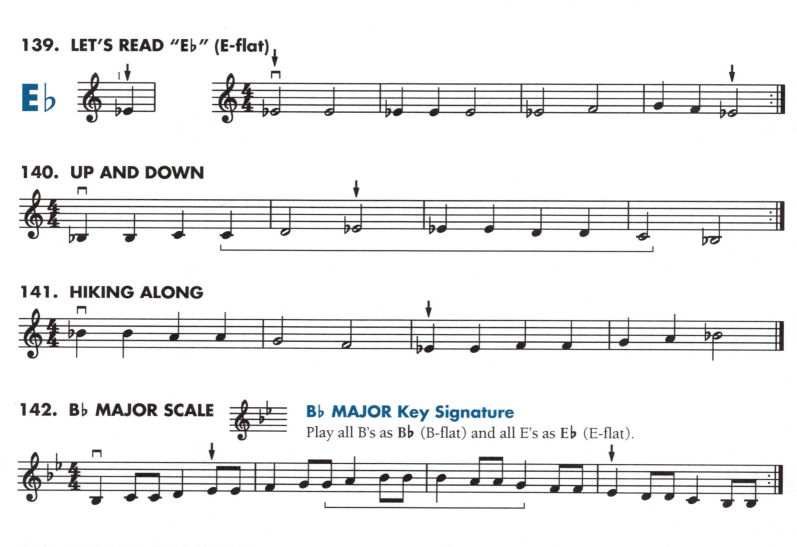

History

Henry Carey (1689-1743) was an English dramatist, poet, and composer. No. 144. *America* is based upon his melody "God Save The Queen", which became popular in the 1790s in England because of the British king's ill health and the Napoleonic wars. The year Carey died, Thomas Jefferson was born and Voltaire wrote *Mérope*.

144. AMERICA
Henry Carey

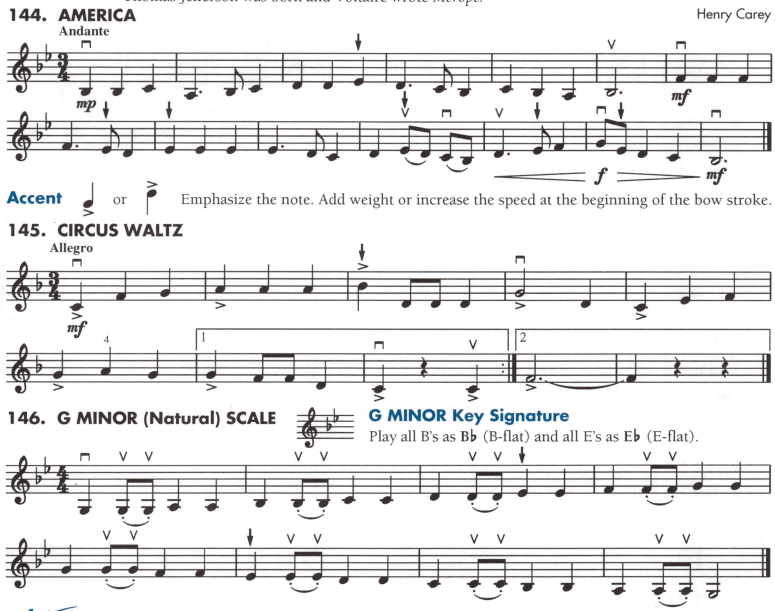

Accent ♩> or ♩^ Emphasize the note. Add weight or increase the speed at the beginning of the bow stroke.

145. CIRCUS WALTZ

146. G MINOR (Natural) SCALE

G MINOR Key Signature
Play all B's as B♭ (B-flat) and all E's as E♭ (E-flat).

History

With the establishment of Israel as an independent political state in 1948, *Hatikvah* became the Israeli National Anthem. Israeli violinists Itzhak Perlman and Pinchas Zukerman are concert artists known throughout the world. The same year Israel became a state, Mohandas Gandhi was assassinated in India.

147. ESSENTIAL ELEMENTS QUIZ - HATIKVAH
Israeli National Anthem

A NEW FINGER PATTERN - Low 4th Finger

Step 1 - Shape your left hand as shown. Be certain your palm faces you. Notice that your 3rd and 4th fingers lightly touch.

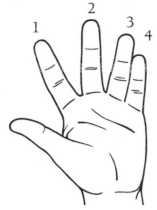

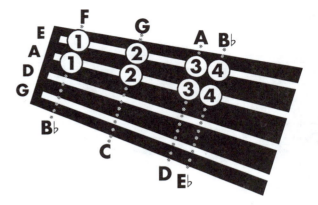

Step 2 - Bring your hand to the fingerboard. Your 3rd and 4th fingers touch. There is a space between your 1st and 2nd fingers, and between your 2nd and 3rd fingers.

E♭

is played with low 4th finger on the A string.

B♭

is played with low 4th finger on the E string.

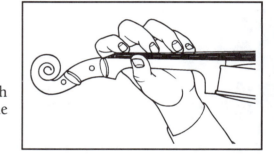

Listening Skills — Play what your teacher plays. Listen carefully.

148. LET'S READ "E♭" (E-flat)

149. LET'S READ "B♭" (B-flat)

150. B♭ MAJOR SCALE

151. REACHING HIGHER Remember to count.

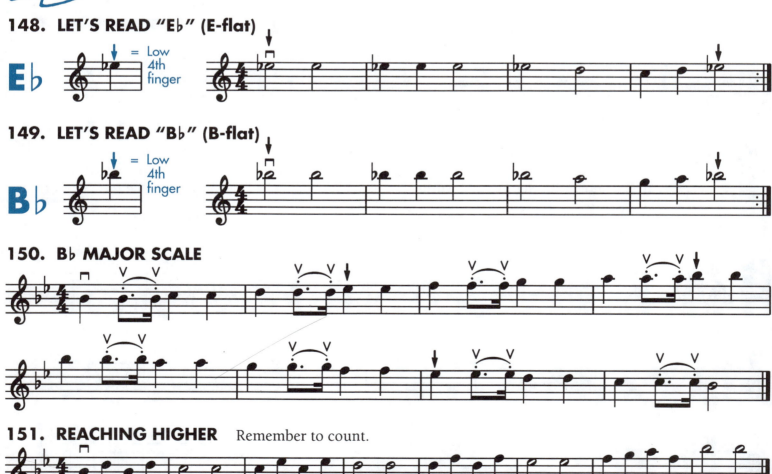

Team Work Great musicians give encouragement to their fellow performers. Viola and cello players will now learn a new challenging skill. The success of your orchestra depends on everyone's talent and patience. Play your best as members of these sections advance their musical technique.

 Play what your teacher plays. Listen carefully.

152. LET'S READ "E♭" (E-flat) - Review

153. MOVING ALONG

154. BELLS OF BLUE

155. SAKURA, SAKURA

Japanese Folk Song

Time Signature (Meter)   Cut Time (Alla Breve)   ¢ or **2/2** - 2 beats per measure - ♩ or ‑ gets one beat

o	= 2 beats
♩	= 1 beat
♪	= 1/2 beat

156. RHYTHM RAP

157. A CUT ABOVE

158. CUT TIME DOODLE

Moderato

159. GOOD KING WENCESLAS

English Carol

Allegretto

▲ Same as ¢

rit.

160. ANCHORS AWEIGH

Charles A. Zimmerman

Allegro

mf

mp   cresc.   f

f

161. RING THE BELLS

Black American Spiritual

Allegretto

mf   1 & 2 &

162. ESSENTIAL ELEMENTS QUIZ - TO A WILD ROSE

Edward MacDowell

163. RHYTHM RAP

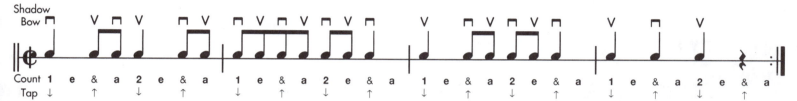

164. DOWN HOME

165. COUNTRY JAM - Orchestra Arrangement

John Higgins

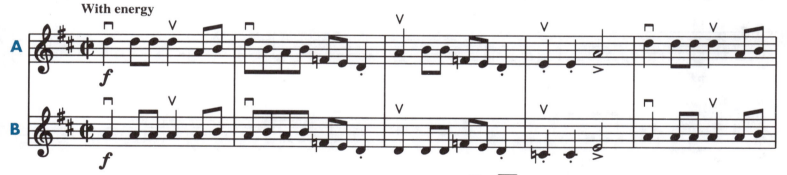

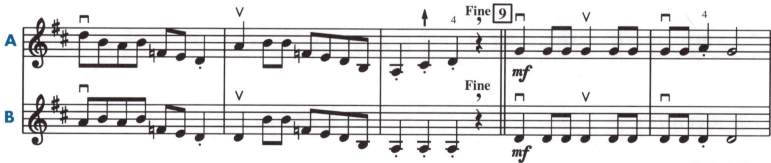

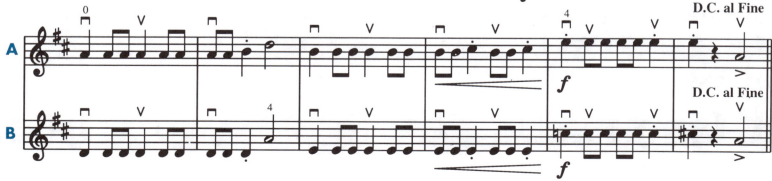

38

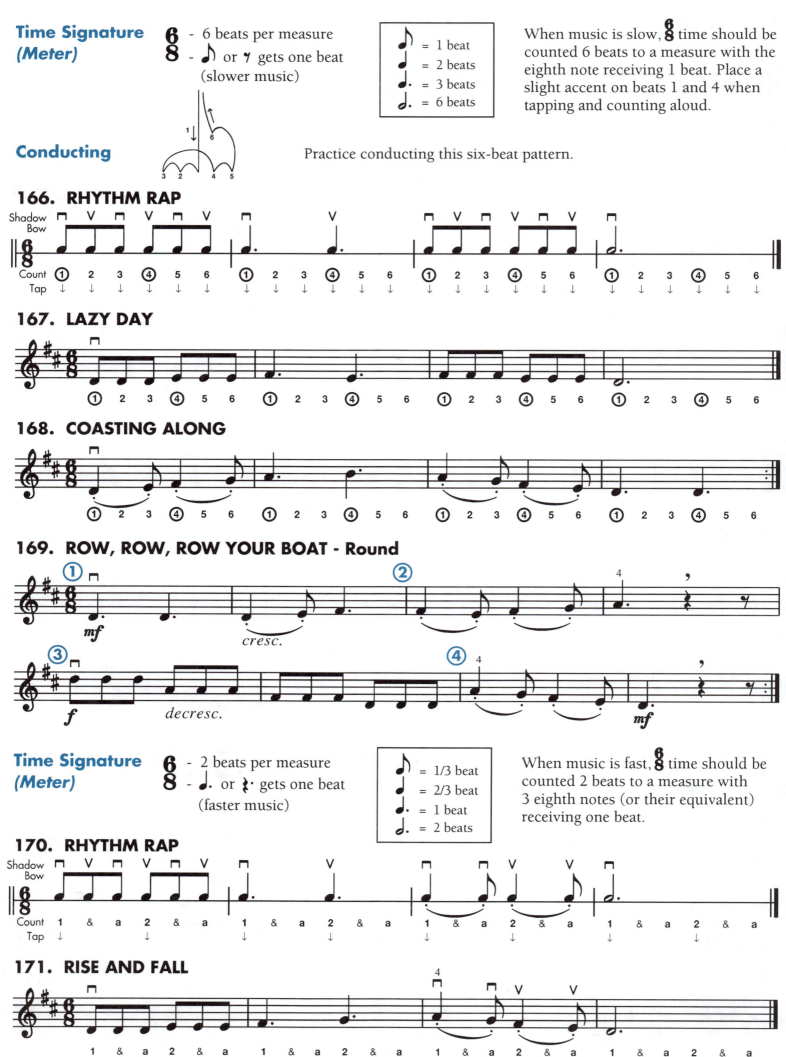

Time Signature (Meter)

6 - 6 beats per measure
8 - ♪ or 𝄾 gets one beat (slower music)

♪	= 1 beat
♩	= 2 beats
♩.	= 3 beats
𝅗𝅥.	= 6 beats

When music is slow, **6/8** time should be counted 6 beats to a measure with the eighth note receiving 1 beat. Place a slight accent on beats 1 and 4 when tapping and counting aloud.

Conducting

Practice conducting this six-beat pattern.

166. RHYTHM RAP

167. LAZY DAY

168. COASTING ALONG

169. ROW, ROW, ROW YOUR BOAT - Round

Time Signature (Meter)

6 - 2 beats per measure
8 - ♩. or 𝄾. gets one beat (faster music)

♪	= 1/3 beat
♩	= 2/3 beat
♩.	= 1 beat
𝅗𝅥.	= 2 beats

When music is fast, **6/8** time should be counted 2 beats to a measure with 3 eighth notes (or their equivalent) receiving one beat.

170. RHYTHM RAP

171. RISE AND FALL

172. JOLLY GOOD FELLOW

173. WHEN JOHNNY COMES MARCHING HOME
Remember to count.　　Patrick Gilmore

174. ESSENTIAL ELEMENTS QUIZ - OVER THE RIVER

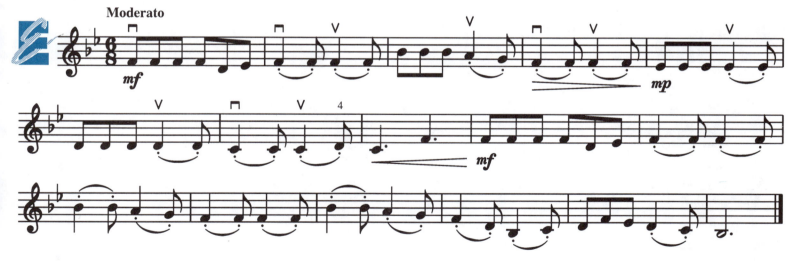

175. SIGHTREADING CHALLENGE #13
Review the **STARS** guidelines before sightreading.

40

Triplets A triplet is a group of three notes. In ²₄, ³₄, or ⁴₄ time, an eighth note triplet is played in one beat.

176. RHYTHM RAP

177. TRIPLET TUNE

178. G MAJOR SCALE WITH TRIPLETS

179. THEME FROM FAUST

Charles Gounod

Moderato

180. MARCH FROM THE NUTCRACKER - Duet

Tchaikovsky

Allegretto

Double Stops — Playing two strings at once.

181. TWO AT A TIME

182. DOUBLE DUTY

183. ADDING FINGERS

184. TRICKY TUNNELS

Bariolage

A bowing style where no two notes in a row are played on the same string. This can involve two, three, or four strings. Practice the following two lines slowly with single bows. Then try adding two and four note slurs.

185. STRING CROSSING

186. CROSS OVER AGAIN

Improvisation

The art of performing music freely, creating your own melody as you play.

187. YOU NAME IT

Make up your own melody to go with the accompaniment line. Don't write it in, so that you can play a different melody next time.

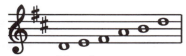

Use these notes to make up a melody.   Accompaniment

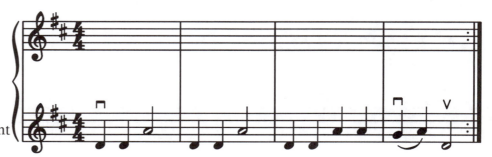

42

INTRODUCING THIRD POSITION

Shape your hand on the D string as shown. Note the placement of your 1st finger when in third position (III).

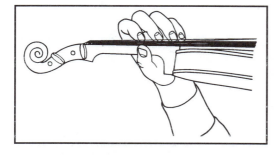

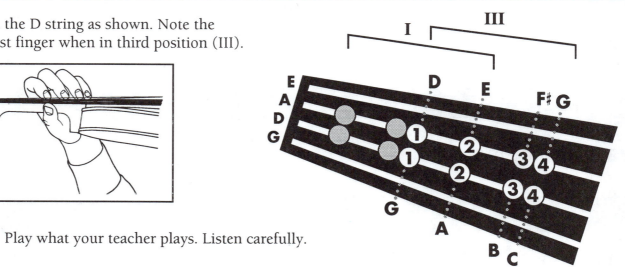

Listening Skills Play what your teacher plays. Listen carefully.

188. NEW POSITION

Locate 1st finger in third position on the D string.

189. SMOOTH SAILING

190. STARTING HIGHER

Locate 1st finger in third position on the A string.

191. OZARK CROSSING

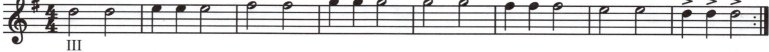

192. SUMMER SUNRISE

193. IN REVERSE

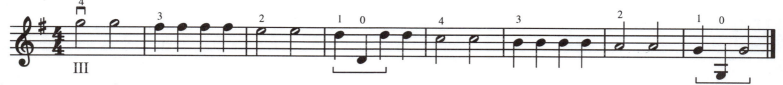

194. A SONG FOR ANNE

Moderato

THIRD POSITION ON THE E STRING

Shape your hand on the E string as shown.

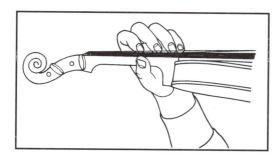

 Play what your teacher plays. Listen carefully.

195. STILL HIGHER

Locate 1st finger in third position on the E string.

New notes: C♯   D

196. D MAJOR SCALE (In third position)

197. SKY HIGH

Shifting   Sliding your left hand smoothly and lightly to a new location on the fingerboard, indicated by a dash (–). Be sure your thumb moves with your hand.

198. TRYING IT OUT

199. SHIFT AGAIN   Remember to count.

200. TWO TO ONE

44

201. C MAJOR SCALE AND ARPEGGIO

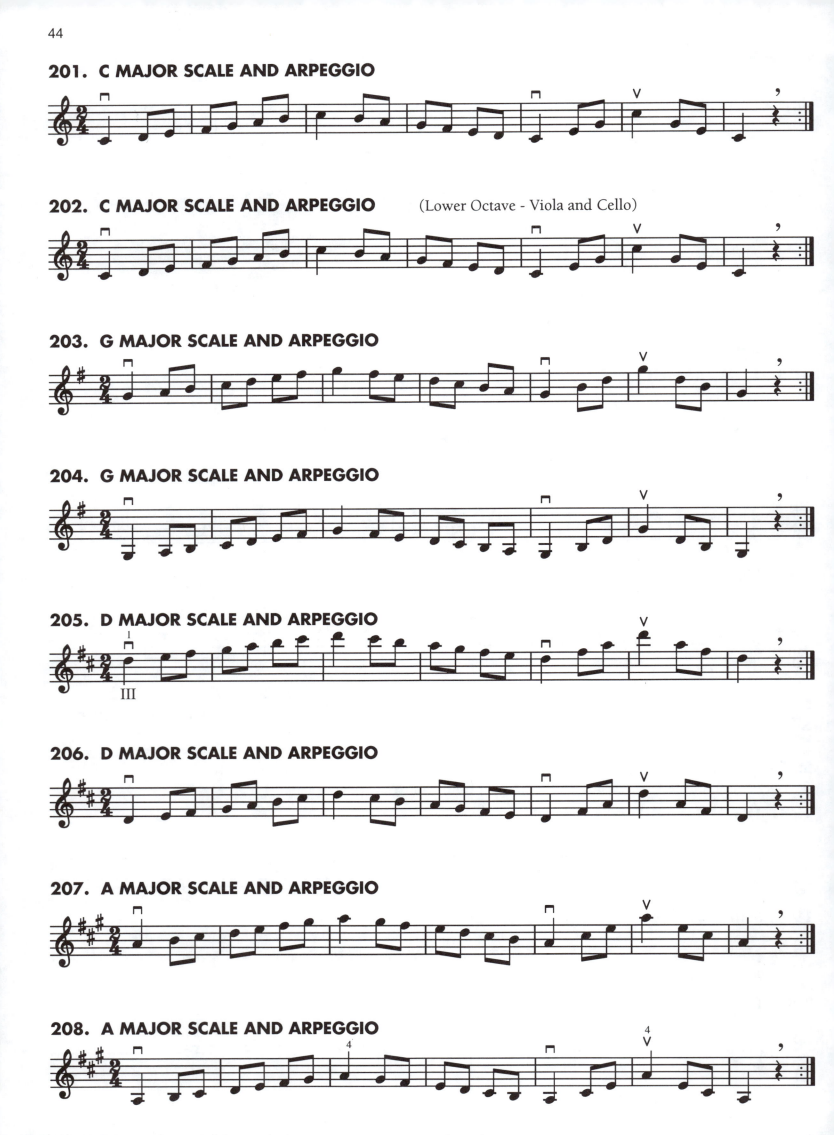

202. C MAJOR SCALE AND ARPEGGIO (Lower Octave - Viola and Cello)

203. G MAJOR SCALE AND ARPEGGIO

204. G MAJOR SCALE AND ARPEGGIO

205. D MAJOR SCALE AND ARPEGGIO

206. D MAJOR SCALE AND ARPEGGIO

207. A MAJOR SCALE AND ARPEGGIO

208. A MAJOR SCALE AND ARPEGGIO

45

209. F MAJOR SCALE AND ARPEGGIO

210. B♭ MAJOR SCALE AND ARPEGGIO

211. B♭ MAJOR SCALE AND ARPEGGIO

212. D MINOR (Natural) SCALE AND ARPEGGIO

213. D MINOR (Natural) SCALE AND ARPEGGIO   (Lower Octave - Viola and Cello)

214. G MINOR (Natural) SCALE AND ARPEGGIO

215. G MINOR (Natural) SCALE AND ARPEGGIO

216. GREENSLEEVES - Orchestra Arrangement

English Folk Song
Arr. John Higgins

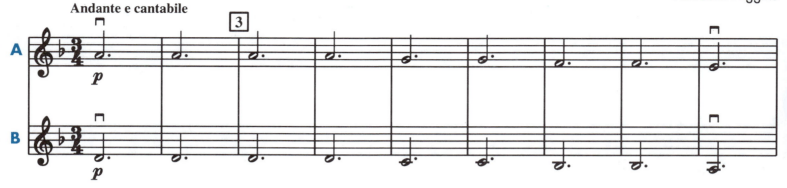

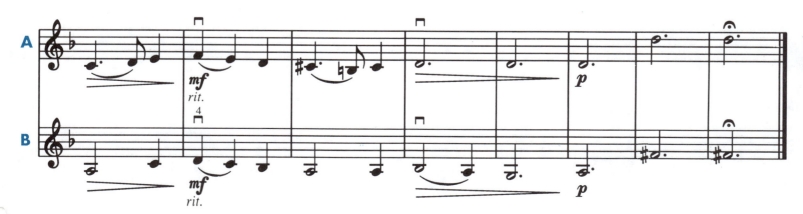

Composition

The process of creating music.

Finish the following example by composing a musical idea.
(Don't forget the title!)

217. _____

VIOLIN FINGERING CHART

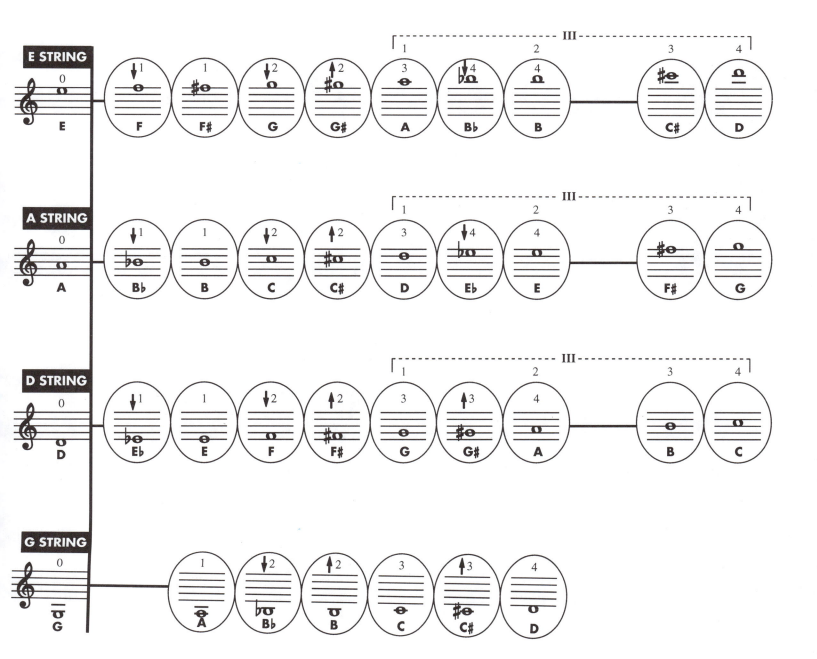

GLOSSARY and INDEX

Essential Element	Definition	Essential Element	Definition
A Tempo	Return to original tempo. (p. 19)	Hooked Bowing	Two or more notes played in the same bow direction with a pause in between.
Accent	Emphasize the note. (p. 33)	Improvisation	The art of performing music freely, creating your own melody as you play. (p. 41)
Accidental	Natural, sharp or flat not in key signature. Remains in effect for the full measure.	Interval	Distance between two notes. (p. 2)
Allegretto	A lively tempo. (p. 5)	Intonation	How well each note is played in tune. (p. 4)
Allegro	Fast bright tempo.	Key Change	When a key signature changes in the middle of a piece of music. (p. 11)
Andante	Slow walking tempo.	Legato	Play in a smooth and connected style. (p. 10)
Andantino	A tempo that is slightly quicker than *Andante*. (p. 9)	Lento	A very slow tempo. (p. 15)
Arco *arco*	Play with the bow on the instrument.	Mahler, Gustav	German composer (1860-1911). (p. 16)
Arpeggio	A chord whose pitches are played one at a time.	Major Scale	Series of 8 notes that follow a definite pattern of whole steps and half steps. (p. 2)
Bach, Johann Sebastian	German composer (1685-1750). (p. 24)	Meter Change	A meter (time signature) change in music. (p. 20)
Bariolage	A bowing style where no two notes in a row are played on the same string. (p. 41)	*mezzo forte* **mf**	Play moderately loud. (p. 4)
Bow Lift	Lift the bow and return to its starting point.	*mezzo piano* **mp**	Play moderately soft. (p. 4)
Cantabile	In a singing style. (p. 22)	Minor Scale	Series of 8 notes which follow a definite pattern of whole steps and half steps. (p. 16)
Cantata	Pieces much like short operas that were written during the Baroque Period (1600-1750). (p. 24)	Moderato	Moderate tempo.
Carey, Henry	English composer (1689-1743). (p. 33)	Natural Sign	Cancels sharps or flats and remains in effect for the full measure.
Chorale	German hymn or song. (p. 9)	*piano* **p**	Play softly.
Composition	The process of creating music. (p. 47)	Pizzicato *pizz.*	Pluck the strings.
Concerto	A composition in several movements for solo instrument and orchestra. (p. 13)	Purcell, Henry	English composer (1659-1695). (p. 29)
Crescendo	Gradually increase volume. (p. 3)	Quarter Note	One beat of sound.
Cut Time	Meter in which the half note gets one beat. (p. 36)	Quarter Rest	One beat of silence.
D.C. al Fine	Play until D.C. al Fine, go back to beginning, and play until you see Fine.	Repeat Sign	Go back to beginning and play the music again.
Decrescendo	Gradually decrease volume. (p. 3)		Repeat the section of music enclosed by the repeat sign.
Dotted Half Note	Three beats of sound.	Ritardando *(ritard.) (rit.)*	Gradually slow the tempo. (p. 3)
Dotted Quarter Note	One and one-half beats of sound. (p. 8)	Shadow Bowing	Bowing without the instrument.
Double Stops	Playing two strings at once. (p. 41)	Sharp	Raises the sound of note(s) a half step.
Down Bow	Move bow away from your body.	Shifting	Sliding your left hand to a new location on the fingerboard. (p. 43)
e	The Italian word for "and". (p. 10)	Sightreading	Playing a musical selection for the first time. (p. 7)
Eighth Note	One-half beat of sound.	Sixteenth Notes	Four sixteenth notes = One beat of sound. (p. 26)
Eighth Rest	One-half beat of silence. (p. 6)	Slur	Curved line that connects two or more different pitches.
Fermata	Hold the note longer. (p. 8)	Staccato	Shortened note. Play with stopped bow stroke.
1st and 2nd Endings	Play the 1st ending the 1st time, skip to 2nd ending on repeat.	Syncopation	Emphasis on the weak beats of the music. (p. 30)
Flat	Lowers the sound of note(s) a half step.	Tie	Curved line that connects notes of the same pitch.
forte **f**	Play loudly.	Triplet	Group of three notes. (p. 40)
Half Note	Two beats of sound.	Up Bow	Move bow toward your body.
Half Rest	Two beats of silence.	Whole Note	4 beats of sound.
Half Step	Smallest distance between two notes.	Whole Rest	4 beats of silence.
Harmony	Two or more different pitches sounding at the same time.	Whole Step	Two half steps.
Haydn, Franz Joseph	Austrian composer (1732-1809). (p. 9)		
Holst, Gustav	British composer (1874-1934). (p. 17)		